Super foods

recipes

igloobooks

Published in 2016
by Igloo Books Ltd
Cottage Farm
Sywell
NN6 0BJ
www.igloobooks.com

Cover designed by Charles Wood-Penn
Designed by Charles Wood-Penn
Edited by Natalie Baker

Cover image © iStock / Getty

LEO002 0316
2 4 6 8 10 9 7 5 3 1
ISBN: 978-1-78557-339-2

Printed and manufactured in China

Contents

Introduction

Eating well is not only important for our health, it supports our well-being and encourages others to eat responsibly, too. The foundation for the recipes in this book is a Mediterranean-style diet emphasizing fruits and vegetables, wholegrains and legumes. Some recipes add poultry, fish or meat for heartiness and additional protein. Healthy fats, flavourful and low-fat dairy foods, plus herbs and spices can also be used to give dishes bold flavours. The recipes are simple, fresh and tasty and use easily-sourced ingredients. This is not a diet book. It is about good, nutritious food that nourishes the body and mind.

Superfood for life

The recipes in this book feature short ingredient lists and sensible prep times. In some dishes, a combination may be unexpected or give a simple ethnic twist to healthy ingredients. Sharing good times is also part of well-being, so this is food that brings people together with pleasure. Good eating means enjoying variety – a bit of everything in moderation – rather than following strict rules for what you should eat and what to avoid.

What is good for you can also be good for the planet and your community, so it's great to buy from local farmers and producers where possible, including those who treat livestock humanely. This book aims to be a source of helpful, health-supporting information about a whole range of superfoods and dishes that will become favourites that your family and friends look forward to sharing.

Dark Greens

The strong flavour and deep colour of these leafy greens means that they offer big health benefits. All are rich in carotenes and carotenoids. Cruciferous greens also contain important sulphur compounds.

Chard

Cook the shiny leaves and creamy stems of Swiss chard separately to enjoy its earthy, tender, carotene-rich leaves plus mild-tasting, fibre-rich crunch. The leaves cook like spinach and the stems may be braised or boiled, then sautéed.

Collard greens

This soul food contains as much calcium in a serving as a glass of milk. It is also a powerhouse combination of sulphur compounds. For the sweetest flavour, steam or blanch the shredded leaves, then sauté or braise them with garlic or bacon.

Kale

Among crucifers, kale beats broccoli in beta-carotene and carotenoid content as well as in vitamin A and calcium. There are many types of kale. More tender types can be used for salads and all can be quickly and lightly braised in broth or wine for an easy and healthy side dish.

Mustard greens

There are two types of mustard greens. The first has sharp-tasting, big, ruffled leaves, which have a high calcium content. These are best braised. The second kind, milder-tasting Asian varieties, have smaller leaves that are tender enough to stir-fry.

Spinach

A top source of heart-protective folate, carotenoids, iron and bone-strengthening vitamin K, spinach is incredibly versatile. Spinach can replace lettuce on a sandwich, or be mixed into meatloaf.

Roots, Tubers and Stalks

These roots and tubers, plus asparagus, an above-ground stalk, offer pleasingly assertive or sweet flavours. Most are good both cooked and served raw. Some contain enough sugar to satisfy your sweet tooth naturally. They all contain a useful amount of fibre.

Asparagus

One cup of asparagus provides as much fibre as a slice of multigrain bread. This fibre includes a particular kind that supports good bacteria in your gut. Asparagus is also an excellent source of vitamins A and K.

Beetroot

The pigment that colours beetroot helps detoxify your body. Shredded raw beets can be served as a salad. Also try beet tops, which taste like Swiss chard. Steam them and serve drizzled with olive oil and lemon juice.

Carrots

Carotenoids and cholesterol-lowering fibre make carrots good for more than just your eyes. They are second only to beetroot in sugar content. Their fibre helps your body absorb this sweetness gradually. Serve raw, stir-fried, sautéed or roasted.

Radishes

Actually part of the brassica family, these roots are rich in vitamin C, folic acid and a host of minerals. Radishes' peppery bite is best preserved by eating them raw, and they can be added to salads or sandwiches or eaten on their own with a sprinkle of sea salt. To tame their taste, they can be steamed or sautéed.

Sweet potatoes

The amount of vitamins A, C, B6, manganese, potassium and beta-carotene in sweet potatoes varies, depending on whether their flesh is cream-coloured, yellow or deep red-orange. Bake sweet potatoes, then stir their soft flesh with a fork to enjoy the healthiest mashed potatoes.

Berries and Grapes

Berries and grapes are so loaded with antioxidants that eating them daily is a smart practice. Include them in savoury or sweet cooking in addition to eating them raw.

Blackberries

These plump berries are loaded with fibre. To use them regularly, top pancakes with blackberries simmered along with a little sugar, and include them with other berries when making a cobbler, crumble or pie.

Blueberries

Blueberries are a powerful source of antioxidants that have been linked to improved memory. In addition, they are rich in flavonoids, which contribute to heart health. Versatile, low in calories and high in fibre, they are a must-have for a healthy lifestyle.

Cranberries

Cranberries get their sour taste from tannins, substances also found in red wine and tea. To eat cranberries year-round while using less sugar, include dried cranberries in salads or alongside fresh or frozen ones in sauces, relish and other dishes.

Grapes and raisins

Red and black grapes are the best choice – their skin contains the same health-supporting compounds found in red wine. Since both grapes and raisins are high in sugar, minimize snacking on them in favour of adding them to cereals, salads and desserts.

Raspberries

Raspberries are amazingly rich in fibre, together with an abundance of antioxidants. Fresh berries are delicate and best served the day you buy them. If you must store them, spread them on a paper towel-lined baking tray in one layer before refrigerating.

Strawberries

Strawberries contain lots of vitamin C and a good amount of fibre. They are often a big hit with kids, so keep them on hand for healthy snacking.

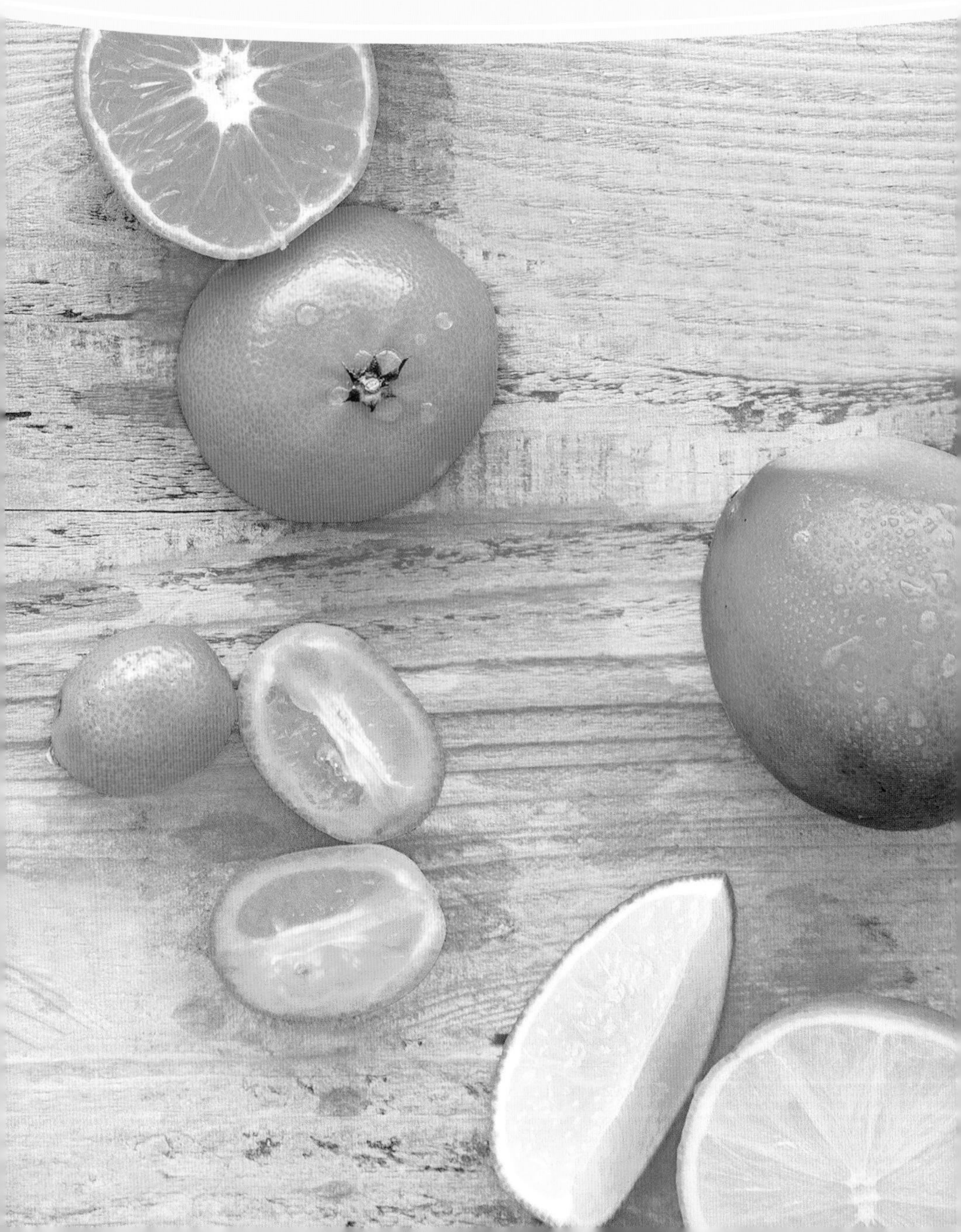

Citrus

To perfume a room, simply peel any citrus fruit. The fragrant oils abundant in their skin also provide valuable health benefits. This makes including their juice or zest in recipes a good idea. Nearly every kind of citrus contains compounds that are unique, so eat a variety of them. Most fruits are at their peak in winter and spring.

Clementines

Clementines are smaller than oranges and have a deeper colour. They are mostly seedless and easy to peel, making them popular with kids. A great snack, clementines are rich in vitamin C, calcium and potassium.

Lemons

A touch of lemon juice or zest gives nearly any dish a flavour boost. The health benefits of lemons are numerous – they can boost your immune system, ease indigestion and calm fever. Home-made lemonade is an easy and refreshing way to gain some of these benefits.

Limes

Limes are an excellent source of vitamin C and a good source of folic acid, vitamin B6, potassium and phytochemicals. Squeeze limes liberally into drinks and use to flavour and finish Asian and Latin American dishes whenever you can.

Oranges

Along with an abundance of vitamin C and potassium, oranges are particularly rich in flavonoids, active compounds found mostly in citrus fruits.

Wholegrains

Studies show that few people eat enough fibre. Serving wholegrains every day is an important – and delicious – way to change this. Their protein and the full feeling you get from eating them make wholegrains fundamental to a plant-based diet.

Brown rice

Brown wholegrain rice is a gluten-free staple in healthy eating. Fluffy brown jasmine and basmati have the same aromatic flavour as white. Nutty-tasting long-grain brown rice has more body. Medium-grain brown rice has a pleasing chewy texture.

Bulgar

Middle Eastern cooks use bulgar – whole wheat that has been steamed, dried and cracked – to make tabbouleh. Its pronounced flavour is also good in pilafs served alongside a main course.

Oats

In the morning, serve rolled oats, thick-cut old-fashioned oats, or nubbly steel-cut oats for breakfast. Use regular or quick-cooking oatmeal – both provide the same amounts of healthy soluble and insoluble fibre.

Quinoa

Light-textured and mildly earthy tasting, quinoa cooks in just 20 minutes. Particularly high in protein, this South American grain makes a good hot breakfast cereal, savoury pilafs and satisfying salads. Red quinoa used in place of bulgar makes great gluten-free tabbouleh.

Lean Protein

Protein is essential for maintaining muscle and helping to repair your body. Besides eating lean cuts of poultry, beef or pork, aim to have fish or seafood at least twice a week. When grilling any type of protein, marinating it first helps to prevent the formation of toxic substances in addition to adding flavour and moisture.

Beef

Eating lean beef in moderation provides needed vitamin B-12, zinc and iron. When it is grass-fed, beef also contains omega-3 fats and is leaner than corn-fed, conventionally raised beef. Combine beef with lots of vegetables for a healthy dish.

Pork

Only turkey breast is leaner than pork tenderloin. To help keep this tender cut moist, roast it whole or sauté it in medallions and serve it with a quick pan sauce.

Poultry

Chicken's white meat is more versatile, but turkey breast has more flavour. Turkey is also slightly leaner and it has less saturated fat than chicken.

Salmon

Wild salmon is the food richest in omega-3 fats. However, the health benefits from salmon are so important that many experts agree that eating farmed is worthwhile if that better suits your budget.

White fish

The mild flavour and adaptability of cod and halibut in cooking help to make eating fish a couple of times a week appealing. Tiny anchovies are also considered sustainable and boast omega-3 fatty acids and some calcium.

Dairy

Eggs, milk, yogurt and cheese are well-priced sources of complete protein, but choosing dairy products with low amounts of saturated fat is best. Eating dairy foods is also the easiest way to get the calcium you need. Including a small amount of strongly flavoured cheese in grain and bean dishes complements their protein and gives a flavour boost.

Buttermilk

Buttermilk is made by culturing low-fat or skimmed milk with friendly bacteria. Buttermilk lightens pancakes, waffles and dessert batters and adds a pleasant tang. Use it to make lean, fluffy mashed potatoes and smart, creamy salad dressings.

Eggs

A whole egg provides 6 grams of top-quality protein. The white contains half an egg's protein, while the rest is in the yolk, along with brain-protecting choline. The yolk's colour comes from carotenoids, which are important for eye health. Using eggs laid by free-range hens supports humane treatment.

Milk

A cup of milk delivers nearly one-third of the calcium an adult needs daily for healthy bones, plus vitamins D and K and magnesium that help your body use it. Using semi-skimmed and skimmed milk saves calories and significantly reduces saturated fat.

Yogurt

To keep your gut happy and healthy, yogurt must deliver cultures that are both live and active. Drink yogurt in a smoothie, combine it with cucumber and mint for a refreshing sauce, or add a dollop of Greek-style yogurt to soups and fruit-based desserts.

Fresh Herbs

The same phytochemical compounds that give herbs their fragrance and flavour also give them proven health benefits. In cooking, use an array of herbs to get the full variety of their powers. Dried herbs quickly lose fragrance and flavour, so use fresh when possible.

Basil

Sweet, spicy Genovese basil and pungent Thai basil with its complex citrus, anise and mint notes are both rich in antimicrobial and anti-inflammatory benefits. Add basil late in the cooking process to preserve the aromas and get full flavour.

Coriander

Widely used in Mexico, the Middle East and South Asian cooking, coriander is rich in antioxidants, plus antimicrobials that can protect against salmonella. Sprinkle it on sliced oranges and on buttery carrots. Heat diminishes its flavour so add it later in chilli and other cooked dishes.

Mint

Sweet, mild spearmint is soothing, while bitter, sharp peppermint is stimulating. Both help to protect against the bacteria associated with ulcers.

Oregano

This Mediterranean staple, which gives familiar flavour to Italian tomato sauce and Greek salad, has the highest antioxidant level of all herbs. When fresh oregano leaves are tough, use dried instead.

Parsley

A main ingredient in tabbouleh and Italian salsa verde, parsley can also be used to make gremolata by combining it with garlic, citrus zest and capers to serve sprinkled on baked fish or lamb shanks.

Working with Herbs

In general, only the leaves from fresh herbs are used in cooking. Below are some tips for how to prep your herbs and get the best results in your dishes.

Large-leafed herbs

Herbs with large or broad leaves, such as basil, sage and mint, can be either slivered or chopped for recipes. Stack 5 or 6 leaves on top of one another, then roll the stack lengthwise into a tight cylinder. Using a chef's knife, cut the leaves crosswise into narrow slivers. To chop the herbs, gather the slivers into a pile and rock the blade over them to cut into small pieces.

Small-leafed herbs

For herbs such as coriander, parsley and tarragon, heap the leaves together on a cutting board. Rock the blade of a chef's knife back and forth briefly over the leaves to chop coarsely. For finely chopped herbs, continue to re-gather the leaves and rock the knife over them making small, even pieces. For minced, keep chopping until the pieces are as fine as possible.

Branched or woody herbs

Remove the petal-like leaves from thyme or oregano by gently pulling your thumb and index finger together down the stems. Gather the leaves on a cutting board and follow the instructions for Small-leafed Herbs (above) to chop or mince.

General tips

- Choose bunches with bright green, fragrant leaves
- Avoid bunches with wilted or discoloured leaves, or pluck these from your garden plot
- Rinse herbs just before using and pat dry gently with paper towels

Spices

Fragrant and vibrantly coloured, spices have potent health benefits. To maximize their benefits, whenever possible, purchase spices whole and then grind them just before use. Buy spices in the smallest amounts you can, as they lose flavour, fragrance and nutrients over time.

Cayenne

Most cayenne pepper registers 35,000–50,000 on the Scoville (or heat) scale – hot, but not incendiary. If you don't like a lot of heat, a tiny pinch of cayenne pepper simply brightens the flavour in many types of dishes.

Cinnamon

Cinnamon's distinctive flavour and fragrance works well in both sweet and savoury dishes. It also helps to control blood sugar levels.

Cumin

Cumin has a sharp, musky flavour and is used liberally in Indian, North African and Latin cooking. Studies have shown that cumin may boost immune health and enhance digestion and it is a rich source of iron.

Ginger

This warming spice has many health benefits. Asian cooks favour using fresh ginger. Grating it helps it blend into dishes nicely. North African and Middle Eastern recipes usually call for dried.

Paprika

Spanish paprika, called pimentón, is darker and tastes more pungent than the Hungarian kind. Both come in sweet and hot varieties but pimentón has a smoked taste that is great with vegetables.

Turmeric

Turmeric has an unfamiliar, bitter taste, so many cooks blend it with other spices or use curry powder containing turmeric. Add a pinch of turmeric to tomato sauce or a pot of lentils.

Spice Basics

Spices are easy to work with, but require a little care to retain maximum flavour and aroma. To ensure freshness and optimum nutrition, get them from a quality source that has a high turnover.

Toasting spices

To intensify their flavour, put whole spices in a dry frying pan over medium heat. Stir constantly for 30 seconds to 1 minute until the spices are fragrant and a shade or two darker. Pour them onto a plate to stop the cooking and let cool for about 10 minutes before grinding.

Grinding spices

For grinding small quantities of spices, use a mortar and pestle. For larger amounts, use a small electric coffee grinder reserved only for grinding spices. Grind only the amount you need for a recipe.

Cooking with spices

Many recipes call for heating ground spices in a small amount of oil prior to incorporating them into a recipe to bring out their flavour. Called 'blooming', this also helps them to blend more readily with other ingredients.

Storing spices

Keep spices in tightly closed containers in a cool, dark place that is ideally not beside the stove. If you buy spices in bulk, purchase glass spice jars for storing. Whole spices will last for about 1 year. Ground spices keep for about 6 months.

Breakfasts and Brunches

It's often said that breakfast is the most important meal of the day, and if you can start the day with a superfood, so much the better.

You may not have time to make these recipes every day of the week, but if you can spare a few minutes in the morning, you will notice the difference throughout the day. They also make a great healthy weekend or special occasion treat.

Use fresh ingredients wherever possible and don't be afraid to experiment with flavours – if you want to add a bit more or less of an ingredient, or try something completely new, go for it!

Strawberry and Banana Smoothie

Serves: 2

Ingredients

1 ripe banana

125 g / 4 oz / 1 cup strawberries

250 ml / 8 fl. oz / 1 cup cranberry juice

250 g / 8 oz / 1 cup fat-free plain yogurt

2 tbsp whole natural almonds

125 g / 4 oz / ½ cup ice cubes

Method

1. Preheat the oven to 220°C (200°C fan) / 425F / gas 7.

2. Peel and slice the banana. Hull the strawberries and halve them lengthwise.

3. In a blender, combine the banana, strawberries, cranberry juice, yogurt, almonds and ice cubes. Blend until frothy and thoroughly blended.

4. Divide between two tall glasses and serve immediately.

Home-made Granola with Blueberries

Serves: 6

Ingredients

185 g / 6 oz / 2 cups rolled oats

45 g / 1 ½ oz / ½ cup raw wheat germ

30 g / 1 oz / ¼ cup walnuts,
  coarsely chopped

20 g / ¾ oz / ¼ cup sesame seeds

30 g / 1 oz / ¼ cup shredded and sweetened
  coconut

40 g / 1 ¼ oz / ¼ cup raw pumpkin
  seeds, hulled

a pinch of salt

3 tbsp honey

2 tbsp grapeseed or canola oil

1 tsp ground cinnamon

500 g / 16 oz / 2 cups fat-free plain
  Greek-style yogurt

250 g / 8 oz / 2 cups blueberries

Method

1. Preheat the oven to 200°C (180°C fan)
   / 400F / gas 6.

2. In a large bowl, combine the oats, wheat
   germ, walnuts, sesame seeds, coconut,
   pumpkin seeds and salt, then stir to mix.
   Spread the mixture in an even layer on a
   large-rimmed baking tray.

3. Bake for 15 minutes, stirring occasionally,
   until golden. Transfer to a large plate to cool.
   The cooled granola will keep at room
   temperature in an airtight container for up
   to 1 week.

4. In a small saucepan over a low heat,
   combine the honey, oil and cinnamon and
   cook for 2 minutes, stirring, until the mixture
   is warm and well blended. Add half of the
   honey mixture to the bowl with the granola
   and toss to combine and coat thoroughly.
   Add just enough of the remaining honey
   mixture so that the granola clumps.

5. Divide the yogurt among individual bowls.
   Top with the granola and blueberries and
   serve immediately.

Waffles with Honeyed Strawberries

Serves: 4

Ingredients

155 g / 5 oz / 1 cup wholewheat flour

75 g / 2 ½ oz / ½ cup plain (all-purpose) flour

2 tbsp wheat bran

1 tbsp baking powder

1 tsp ground cinnamon

½ tsp fine sea salt

375 ml / 12 fl. oz / 1 ½ cups fat-free milk

2 large eggs

2 tbsp grapeseed or canola oil, plus more
   for brushing

2 tbsp wildflower or orange blossom honey

honeyed strawberries (see p. 39)

Method

1. In a large bowl, whisk together the flours, bran, baking powder, cinnamon and salt. In a large glass measuring pitcher, whisk together the milk, eggs and the oil until blended. Add the honey to the milk mixture and whisk until blended. Make a well in the centre of the dry ingredients and add the milk mixture. Stir until just blended; do not overmix. The batter will be thick.

2. Preheat the oven to 95°C (75°C fan) / 200F / gas ¼.

3. Preheat a waffle iron for 5 minutes, then brush with oil. Ladle about 125 ml / 4 fl. oz / ½ cup of the batter into the centre of the waffle iron and spread with a small spatula to fill all the holes. Close the waffle iron and cook for 4–5 minutes, or according to the manufacturer's directions, until the steam stops escaping from the sides and the top opens easily.

4. Transfer the waffle to a warmed platter and keep warm in the oven. Repeat with the remaining batter. Serve the waffles with the honeyed strawberries.

Four Ways to Use Fresh Strawberries

Fresh strawberries taste best in early spring and summer, but frozen fruit captures their goodness at other times of the year. Stir a teaspoon of honey or sugar into a bowl of sliced fresh berries and watch them create their own syrup.

Honeyed Strawberries

Serves 4

In a small saucepan over low heat, warm 60 ml / 2 fl. oz / ¼ cup orange blossom or wildflower honey for 1 minute, stirring constantly, until thinned but not hot. Remove from the heat. Add 2 tbsp fresh lemon juice and 125 g / 4 oz / 1 cup hulled and sliced strawberries, then stir until blended.

Cover and let stand at room temperature until ready to serve. Serve with pancakes or waffles immediately.

Strawberry Sauce

Makes 500 ml / 16 fl. oz / 2 cups

In a food processor, combine 250 g / 8 oz / 2 cups hulled strawberries and 2–3 tbsp honey (depending on how sweet the berries are) and pulse until the berries are puréed.

Pour the purée through a sieve set over a bowl, pressing the purée with a wooden spoon.

Stir in 1–2 tsp fresh lemon juice, then cover and refrigerate for up to 5 days.

Roasted Berries

Makes about 750 ml / 20 fl. oz / 2 ½ cups

In a wide, shallow baking dish, combine 250 g / 8 oz / 2 cups hulled strawberries with 60 g / 2 oz / ½ cup blueberries, 80 g / 2 fl. oz / ¼ cup maple syrup and 1 tbsp fresh orange juice, then toss to coat. Spread the berries in an even layer. Roast the berries in a 230°C (210°C fan) / 450F / gas 8 oven for 5–7 minutes, until they soften.

Serve warm with crisp, wholegrain cookies or low-fat cake or over low-fat frozen yogurt.

Dark Chocolate-dipped Strawberries

Makes 12–16 dipped strawberries

Place 250 g / 8 oz chopped, dark chocolate in a heatproof bowl. Place over a saucepan of barely simmering water, ensuring the bowl does not touch the water. Heat, until melted. Remove from the heat. Dip each strawberry about two-thirds of the way into the chocolate, then set on a baking tray lined with greaseproof paper. Refrigerate until the chocolate is set; about 15 minutes or up to 2 hours.

Sweet Potato Maple Pancakes

Serves: **6**

Ingredients

2 sweet potatoes, scrubbed but not peeled

2 tbsp unsalted butter

375 ml / 12 fl. oz / 1 ½ cups fat-free milk

2 large eggs

2 tbsp brown sugar

1 ½ tsp pure vanilla extract

155 g / 5 oz / 1 cup wholewheat flour

75 g / 2 ½ oz / ½ cup plain (all-purpose) flour

1 tbsp baking powder

½ tsp ground cinnamon and freshly
   grated nutmeg

½ tsp salt

canola oil spray

60 g / 2 oz / ½ cup walnuts, toasted and
   coarsely chopped

warmed pure maple syrup, to serve

Method

1. Preheat the oven to 95°C (75°C fan) / 200F /
   gas ¼. Pierce the sweet potatoes a few
   times with a fork, then microwave on high
   for 8 minutes, until tender. Split each potato
   lengthwise, then scoop out 185 g / 6 oz /
   1 ¼ cups of the flesh.

2. In a food processor, combine the sweet
   potato flesh with the butter and pulse until
   incorporated. Add 125 ml / 4 fl. oz / ½ cup
   of the milk, the eggs, brown sugar and
   vanilla and pulse until smooth. Transfer
   to a bowl and whisk in the remaining milk.
   In a large bowl, combine the flours, baking
   powder, cinnamon, nutmeg and salt.
   Combine both mixtures and stir until
   combined. Do not overmix.

3. Place a griddle over medium heat until hot
   and coat lightly with canola oil. Pour 60 ml /
   2 fl. oz / ¼ cup of the batter onto the griddle
   and cook for 2 ½ minutes, until bubbles
   break on the surface. Flip the pancakes
   and cook for 2 minutes longer, until golden
   brown. Transfer to a baking tray and keep
   warm in the oven. Repeat.

4. Serve with the walnuts and syrup.

Swiss Chard and Onion Frittata

Serves: 6

Ingredients

1 bunch Swiss chard

4 tbsp olive oil

1 small yellow onion, thinly sliced

salt and freshly ground black pepper

6 large eggs

4 cloves garlic, finely chopped

30 g / 1 oz / ¼ cup Parmesan cheese,
  freshly grated

1–2 pinches cayenne pepper

Method

1. Preheat the oven to 180°C (160°C fan) / 350F / gas 4. Separate the stems from the chard leaves by cutting along both sides of the centre vein. Cut the chard stems crosswise into slices 6 mm (¼ in) thick and coarsely chop the leaves. Set aside.

2. In a large frying pan, heat 2 tbsp of the oil over a medium heat. Add the onion and sauté until tender. Add the chard stems, season with salt and sauté for 4 minutes, until they start to soften. Add the leaves and sauté until all of the chard is tender. Transfer to a plate, then set aside.

3. In a large bowl, lightly beat the eggs with the garlic and Parmesan. Season with cayenne, salt and pepper to taste.

4. Drain the liquid from the plate, then stir into the egg mixture. In a 20 cm (8 in) ovenproof pan, heat the remaining oil over a medium high heat. Add the egg mixture, reduce the heat to medium, then cook for 5 minutes. Oven bake for 7–9 minutes until completely set. Cut the frittata into wedges and serve straight from the pan.

Poached Eggs with Sweet Peppers

Serves: 4

Ingredients

2 tbsp olive oil

1 small yellow onion, thinly sliced

sea salt and freshly ground black pepper

1 clove garlic, minced

1 red, yellow and orange bell pepper,
    deseeded and thinly sliced

2 tbsp white wine vinegar

1 tsp sugar

4 large eggs

2 tbsp fresh flat-leaf parsley, chopped

Method

1. In a frying pan, heat the olive oil over a medium heat. Add the onion and a pinch of salt and pepper. Cook for 4–5 minutes, stirring occasionally, until the onion begins to soften. Add the garlic, peppers and seasoning. Cook for another 6–8 minutes, until the peppers and onion is soft. Stir in 1 tbsp of the vinegar and sugar cooking for 1–2 minutes, until the vinegar has almost evaporated. Cover to keep warm.

2. Fill a deep sauté pan halfway with cold water. Add 1 tsp salt and the remaining vinegar, then place the pan over a medium heat. When the water begins to simmer, break the eggs one at a time into a cup and slip each one into the water. Cook for 1 minute, then gently slide a spatula under the eggs to prevent sticking. Poach for 3–5 minutes.

3. To serve, divide the pepper mixture among individual plates. Using a slotted spoon, scoop the eggs from the simmering water, drain, then place each on top of a serving of peppers. Sprinkle with the parsley and serve immediately.

Huevos Rancheros

Serves: 4

Ingredients

4 wholewheat tortillas

1 tbsp grapeseed or canola oil

4 large eggs

sea salt and freshly ground black pepper

375 ml / 12 fl. oz / 1 ½ cups tomato sauce

250 g / 8 oz / 1 cup fat-free canned refried
black beans, warmed

1 small ripe avocado, halved, pitted, peeled
and sliced

45 g / 1 ½ oz / ⅓ cup crumbled feta cheese

155 g / 5 oz / ⅔ cup fat-free plain Greek-
style yogurt

1 tbsp fresh coriander (cilantro), coarsely
chopped

Method

1. Preheat the oven to 95°C (75°C fan) / 200F
/ gas ¼. Wrap the tortillas in kitchen foil and
warm in the oven.

2. In a large frying pan set over a medium-low
heat, warm the oil. Carefully break the eggs
into the pan and fry slowly for 3 minutes,
until the whites are set and the yolks have
begun to thicken but are not hard. Cover the
frying pan if you like firm yolks. Season to
taste with salt and pepper.

3. To assemble, remove the tortillas from the
oven. Using tongs, dip each tortilla quickly
in the warmed tomato sauce and place on
warmed individual plates.

4. Spread 60 g / 2 oz / ¼ cup of the refried
beans evenly on each tortilla and top each
with a fried egg. Spoon more of the tomato
sauce generously over the eggs and tortilla.
Top with the avocado, cheese, yogurt and
coriander. Serve immediately.

Chicken and Avocado Quesadillas

Serves: 4

Ingredients

olive oil for greasing, plus 1 tbsp

1 small chicken escalope

sea salt and freshly ground black pepper

4 large eggs

60 g / 2 oz / 1 cup spinach, coarsely chopped

1 ripe small tomato, deseeded and chopped

2 wholewheat tortillas

60 g / 2 oz / ½ cup sharp white Cheddar cheese, shredded

60 g / 2 oz / ¼ cup fat-free Greek-style yogurt

1 small ripe avocado, pitted, peeled and sliced

60 g / 2 oz / ¼ cup pico de gallo, or tomato salsa

Method

1. Preheat the grill. Lightly oil a grill pan, then set aside. Brush the chicken with oil and season. Arrange the chicken on the pan and grill for 5 minutes, turning once, until lightly browned on both sides. Cut into 12 mm (½ in) dice.

2. In a bowl, whisk together the eggs, ¼ tsp salt and a pinch of pepper. In a frying pan, heat 1 tbsp olive oil over a medium heat. Add the eggs and scramble until starting to set. Add the chicken, spinach and tomato and continue cooking for another minute, stirring until the eggs are cooked. Remove from the heat and set aside.

3. Heat the frying pan on a medium heat and add the tortilla. Flip the tortilla and sprinkle half of the cheese over the bottom half, then top the cheese with half of the egg-chicken mixture. Fold over the top of the tortilla and cook for 1 minute on each side. Transfer to a baking tray and keep warm in the oven and repeat with the other tortilla.

4. Cut the quesadillas into wedges. Top each serving with yogurt, avocado and pico de gallo or tomato salsa. Serve immediately.

Main Dishes

Before preparing each meal, it's important to consider the vital nutrients we need in order to function well. Ideally, every plate of food should include plenty of fresh vegetables, complex carbohydrates, a portion of protein and healthy fats for a well-balanced tasty dish.

The recipes in this book are designed to nourish and sustain you throughout the day. From warming soups and zesty salads to tender salmon and filling pastas, you'll be spoilt for choice!

Whether you're cooking a modest meal for one, or a feast for the whole family, there are plenty of options to please everyone. These dishes are centred around fresh vegetables and wholegrains, but meat-lovers need not fear – you'll also find a number of dishes that include meat and fish, too.

Roasted Tomato and Onion Soup

Serves: 4–6

Ingredients

1.5 kg / 3 lb ripe tomatoes

2 tbsp olive oil

2 tbsp balsamic vinegar

1 clove garlic, minced

2 tsp fresh thyme leaves

sea salt and freshly ground black pepper

1 yellow onion, chopped

125 ml / 4 fl. oz / ½ cup dry white wine

750 ml / 1 ¼ pints / 3 cups low-sodium chicken broth

2 tbsp fresh flat-leaf parsley, chopped

Method

1. Preheat the oven to 160°C (140°C fan) / 325F / gas 3. Cut the tomatoes in half and place on a baking tray. In a small bowl, whisk together 1 tbsp of the olive oil, vinegar, garlic, thyme, ¼ tsp salt and ¼ tsp pepper. Spoon the mixture evenly over the tomatoes. Roast for 1 hour, until the tomatoes are soft.

2. In a soup pot, heat the remaining olive oil over a medium-high heat. Add the onion and cook for 5–7 minutes, then add the wine, raise the heat to medium-high and cook for 2–3 minutes, until the liquid has evaporated. Stir in the chicken broth and roasted tomatoes. Return to a boil, then reduce the heat to medium-low. Cover and simmer for 10 minutes.

3. In a blender or food processor, pulse the soup until smooth. Return to the pot and season with salt and pepper. Reheat the soup gently over medium heat until hot.

4. Ladle into warmed bowls, garnish with the parsley and serve immediately.

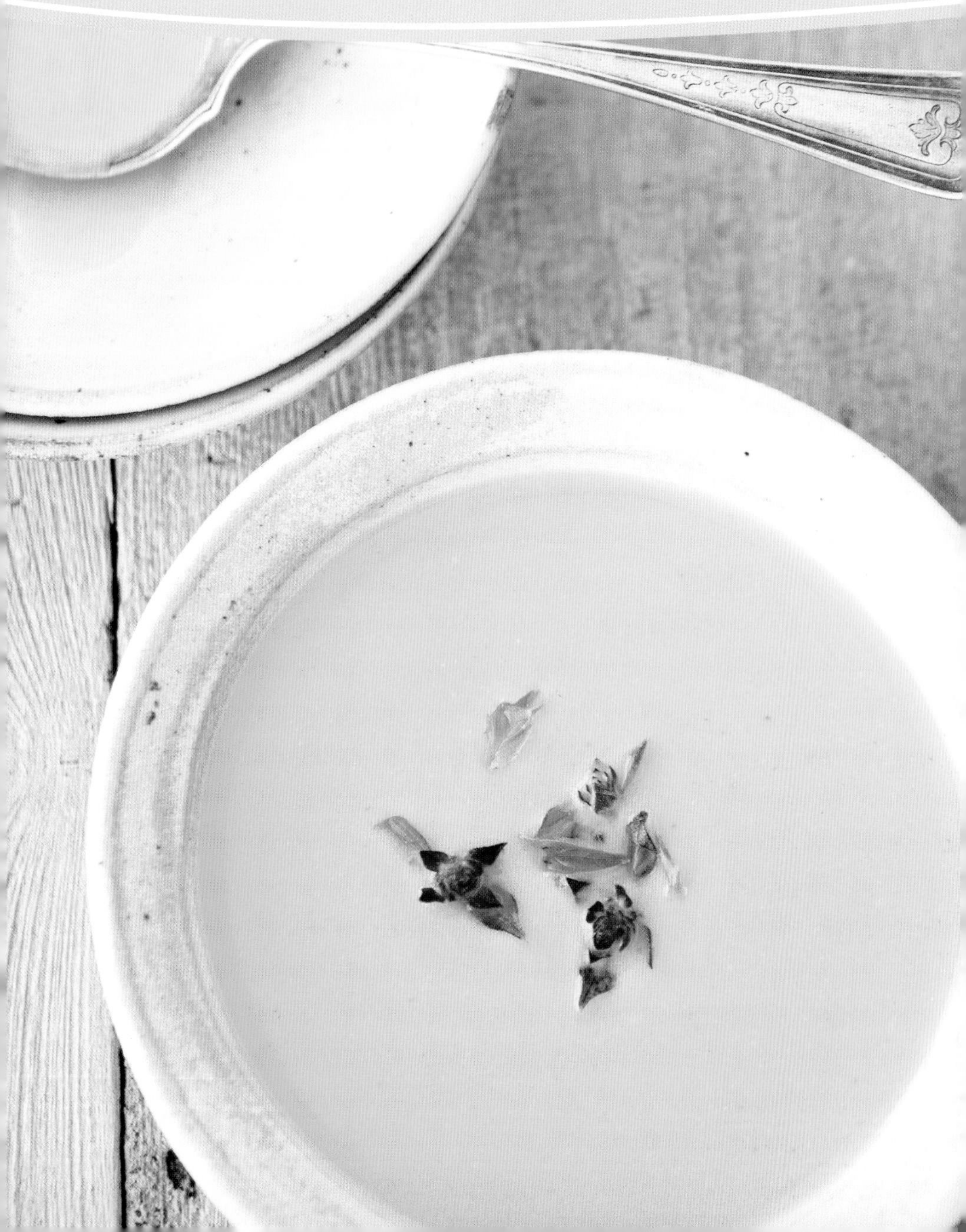

Curried Butternut Squash Soup

Serves: 4

Ingredients

1 large butternut squash

1 ½ tbsp olive oil

4 large shallots, sliced

1 tbsp fresh ginger, peeled and grated

1 clove garlic, minced

750 ml / 1 ¼ pints / 3 cups low-sodium chicken or vegetable broth

sea salt

1 tsp Thai red curry paste

180 ml / 6 fl. oz / ¾ cup light coconut milk

2 tsp fresh lime juice

Method

1. Remove the stem end from the squash, then cut in half lengthwise. Scoop out the seeds and discard. Peel, then cut the flesh into 2.5 cm (1 in) cubes.

2. In a soup pot, heat the olive oil over a medium heat. Add the shallots and cook for 2–3 minutes, until softened. Add the ginger and garlic and cook for 1 minute, until fragrant but not browned. Add the squash, broth and ½ tsp salt and bring to a boil over high heat. Reduce the heat to maintain a simmer, cover and cook for 20 minutes, until the squash is tender. Remove from the heat and cool slightly.

3. In a small bowl, combine the curry paste and coconut milk and whisk until well blended. In a blender or food processor, working in batches if necessary, pulse the soup until smooth. Return to the pot and stir in the curry and coconut milk mixture. Reheat the soup over a medium heat until hot and season with lime juice and salt to taste. Ladle into warmed bowls and serve immediately.

Tuscan-style Bean and Kale Soup

Serves: 8

Ingredients

220 g / 7 oz / 1 cup dried or tinned borlotti
   beans, soaked and drained

1 bunch Tuscan kale

2 tbsp olive oil

1 large yellow onion, chopped

1 large carrot, peeled and chopped

1 celery stick, thinly sliced

2 cloves garlic, minced

875 g / 1 lb 12 oz / 1 can whole
   plum tomatoes

1 bay leaf

a pinch of red pepper flakes

sea salt and freshly ground black pepper

Method

1. Rinse the beans thoroughly under cold
   running water and drain. Place the beans
   in a bowl and soak overnight.

2. Drain the beans and transfer them to a
   soup pot. Bring to a boil over a high heat,
   then simmer for 1–1½ hours until the beans
   are tender. Drain the beans, pouring the
   liquid into a separate bowl and set aside.

3. Separate the stems from the kale leaves.
   Cut the leaves crosswise into strips about
   12 mm (½ in) wide. Discard the stems.

4. In a soup pot, heat the olive oil over a
   medium-high heat. Add the onion, carrot
   and celery and sauté for 5–7 minutes, until
   translucent. Add the kale and stir for about
   5 minutes until wilted. Add the garlic and
   sauté. Pour the tomatoes and their juices
   to the pot and stir to combine.

5. Add the beans and the cooking-liquid
   mixture to the pot along with the bay leaf
   and red pepper flakes. Bring to a boil over
   a medium-high heat, then simmer until the
   beans are cooked through. Season to taste
   and ladle the soup into warm bowls, then
   serve immediately.

Beetroot, Watercress and Egg Salad

Serves: 4

Ingredients

875 g / 1 ¾ lb baby beetroot

6–8 large organic eggs

sea salt and freshly ground black pepper

3 tbsp extra-virgin olive oil

2 tbsp Champagne vinegar

2 tbsp fresh orange juice

1 tsp orange zest, finely grated

125 g / 4 oz watercress, tough stems removed, torn into bite-size pieces

Method

1. Preheat the oven to 200°C (180°C fan) / 400F / gas. Trim the root and stem ends from the beetroot and wrap them in foil. Bake for 1 hour until the beetroot is soft, then unwrap and allow to cool. Peel the beetroot with your fingers or a paring knife. Cut into quarters and place in a bowl.

2. Place the eggs in a saucepan and bring to boil over a medium heat. Remove the pan from the heat, cover, then stand until cooked; about 10 minutes for runny yolks and up to 14 minutes for firm yolks. Drain the eggs, then transfer to a bowl of ice water. Peel the eggs and cut them lengthwise into quarters.

3. In a large bowl, whisk together the oil, vinegar, orange juice, zest and ½ tsp salt to make the dressing. Pour half of the dressing over the beetroot and stir to coat. Separately, combine the watercress and remaining dressing and toss to coat.

4. Mound the watercress on individual plates and top with the beetroot. Arrange the egg quarters around the beetroot and drizzle with the remaining vinaigrette. Sprinkle with a few grindings of pepper and serve.

Pistachio and Chickpea Bulgar Salad

Serves: 6

Ingredients

280 g / 9 oz / 1 ½ cups bulgar wheat

560 ml / 18 fl. oz / 2 ¼ cups vegetable broth

60 ml / 2 fl. oz / ¼ cup fresh lemon juice

60 ml / 2 fl. oz / ¼ cup pomegranate molasses

2 tsp sugar

sea salt and freshly ground black pepper

6 tbsp extra-virgin olive oil

485 g / 15 ½ oz / 1 can chickpeas (garbanzo beans), drained and rinsed

2 large red bell peppers

90 g / 3 oz / ¾ cup shelled roasted pistachio nuts, toasted

20 g / ¾ oz / ½ cup fresh flat-leaf parsley or coriander (cilantro), chopped

125 g / 4 oz / 1 cup dried tart cherries, roughly chopped

Method

1. Put the bulgar in a large heatproof bowl. Bring the broth to boil in a saucepan, then pour it over the bulgar, cover and let stand for about 30 minutes, until the liquid has been absorbed.

2. In a small bowl, whisk the lemon juice, pomegranate molasses, sugar, 1 ½ tsp salt and pepper until the sugar dissolves. Whisk in the oil to make a dressing. In a small bowl, combine the chickpeas and ½ tsp salt. Whisk the dressing, then add it, along with the chickpeas, to the bulgar. Cover and refrigerate for 2 hours.

3. Preheat the grill. Place the peppers on a baking tray. Grill for 10 minutes, turning occasionally, until the skins are charred. Transfer to a bowl and cover for 15 minutes. Remove and discard the skins, stems and seeds and cut the flesh into small dice.

4. Stir together the pistachios and a pinch of salt in a small bowl. Add the pistachios, roasted peppers, parsley and cherries and toss to mix well. Adjust the seasoning to taste, then divide the salad among plates or bowls. Serve immediately.

Quinoa, Lemon and Mint Salad

Serves: 4

Ingredients

375 g / 12 oz / 1 ½ cups quinoa

750 ml / 1 lb 8 oz / 3 cups low-sodium chicken or vegetable broth

sea salt and freshly ground black pepper

2 large lemons

2 cloves garlic, minced

1 tbsp pomegranate molasses

1 tsp sugar

125 ml / 4 fl. oz / ½ cup extra-virgin olive oil

2 ripe large tomatoes, deseeded and diced

½ large cucumber, diced

4 green onions, white and tender green parts, thinly sliced

10 g / ⅓ oz / ¼ cup fresh flat-leaf parsley, coarsely chopped

10 g / ⅓ oz / ¼ cup fresh mint, coarsely chopped

Method

1. Rinse the quinoa and drain. In a saucepan, bring the broth to a boil over a high heat. Add the quinoa and ¼ tsp salt, then reduce the heat. Cover and cook for 15 minutes, until all the water has absorbed and the grains are tender. Transfer to a bowl.

2. Finely grate the zest of 1 lemon, then halve both lemons and juice. In a small bowl, whisk together the lemon juice and zest, garlic, pomegranate molasses, sugar, ½ tsp salt and pepper until the sugar dissolves. Slowly whisk in the oil to make a dressing. Season to taste, then add about three quarters of the dressing to the quinoa and mix well.

3. In a small bowl, toss the tomatoes with ¼ tsp salt and allow to stand for about 5 minutes. Drain in a sieve set over a second bowl. Place the cucumber in the first bowl along with the green onions and remaining dressing. Toss well, then pour the cucumber mixture over the tomatoes in the sieve to drain. Add the drained mixture to the quinoa along with the parsley and mint and mix well. Season to taste and serve immediately.

Spicy Cauliflower Rustic Pasta

Serves: 4

Ingredients

4 slices country-style wholegrain bread

2 cloves garlic, peeled but left whole

2 heads cauliflower

3 tbsp olive oil

sea salt

375 g / ¾ lb / 4 cups wholewheat penne

60 ml / 2 fl. oz / ¼ cup fresh lemon juice

10 g / ⅓ oz / ¼ cup fresh flat-leaf parsley, chopped

3 tbsp capers, drained

1 tsp red pepper flakes

30 g / 1 oz / ¼ cup Parmesan cheese, freshly grated

Method

1. Preheat the oven to 150°C (130°C fan) / 300F / gas 2. Place the bread slices on a baking tray and toast for about 30 minutes, until crisp. Rub one side of each slice with a garlic clove, then tear the bread into chunks. Place the chunks in a food processor and pulse to make coarse crumbs. Set the oven to 200°C (180°C fan) / 400F / gas 6.

2. Cut each cauliflower into quarters, discard any leaves and the cores and roughly chop. Mince the remaining garlic clove. Place the cauliflower in a large baking pan, drizzle with oil, sprinkle with the garlic and ½ tsp salt, then toss to coat. Roast for 20 minutes, turning after 10 minutes, until the cauliflower is brown.

3. Fill a large saucepan with salted water and bring to a boil. Add the pasta to the boiling water and cook for about 12 minutes, until al dente. Drain, reserving 125 ml / 4 fl. oz / ½ cup of the cooking water. Return the pasta to the pot, add the cauliflower, lemon juice, parsley, capers, red pepper flakes and reserved cooking water, then toss to combine. Stir in the breadcrumbs and cheese and serve.

Warm Lentil and Kale Salad

Serves: 6

Ingredients

1 tbsp olive oil

4 carrots, peeled and diced

1 large red onion, thinly sliced

sea salt and freshly ground black pepper

leaves from 1 large bunch Tuscan kale, thinly sliced

220 g / 7 oz / 1 cup brown lentils, rinsed

2 sprigs fresh thyme

4 large cloves garlic

1 l / 32 fl. oz / 4 cups low-sodium chicken broth

6 thin slices prosciutto

1 tsp sherry vinegar

Method

1. Warm the oil in a large saucepan over a medium heat. Add the carrots and onion, ¼ tsp salt and some pepper, then sauté for 15 minutes, until the onion is soft. Add the kale leaves to the saucepan and cook for 6 minutes, stirring occasionally, until tender. Scrape the contents of the pan into a bowl and set aside. Wipe the saucepan clean.

2. In the same saucepan, combine the lentils, thyme, garlic, chicken broth, ½ tsp salt and ¼ tsp pepper and bring to a boil. Reduce the heat to medium and simmer, uncovered, for 15–20 minutes, until the lentils are tender but firm to the bite.

3. In a frying pan over a medium heat, cook the prosciutto for about 7 minutes until brown. Allow to cool, then tear into small pieces.

4. Drain the lentils in the colander. Remove and discard the thyme and garlic, then return the lentils to the saucepan. Stir in the kale mixture, vinegar and ½ tsp salt. Season to taste. Transfer the mixture to a serving bowl, top with the prosciutto and serve.

Four Ways to Use Kale

Ideas abound for using the nutritional powerhouse, kale, such as in a nourishing morning smoothie, as a versatile and simple-to-prepare side dish, stirred into a frittata or pasta sauce, or baked to make crunchy, satisfying crisps as a snack for any time of the day.

Green Smoothie

Serves 4

Using a high-speed blender or masticating vegetable juicer, juice 1 bunch washed kale. Blend the juice into your chosen smoothie, ideally made with fruits, for a healthy elixir to start the day. Or, juice the following in a masticating juicer: 1 pear, 1 apple, 1 bunch kale and 20 g / ¾ oz / ½ cup chopped fresh flat-leaf parsley. Add to a blender along with 125 g / 4 oz / ½ cup ice cubes and 125 ml / 4 fl. oz / ½ cup water; whirl until smooth, then serve.

Wilted Garlicky Greens

Serves 2–3 as a side dish

Remove the stems and tough ribs from 1 bunch kale. Stack the kale leaves on a chopping board, then cut them crosswise into thin strips. Wash the leaves and drain. Warm some olive oil in a large frying pan over a medium-high heat, and add 1–2 cloves minced garlic and ¼ tsp red pepper flakes. Sauté for 1 minute, then add the kale and stir to coat. Add a splash of water to the pan, cover and cook for 5 minutes, until the greens are tender, adding more water if needed.

Frittata or Pasta with Greens

Prepare Wilted Garlicky Greens as directed, then add to your chosen frittata recipe (1 bunch kale is enough for a 6-egg frittata) or add to pasta sauce to enliven a pasta dish (1 bunch kale is sufficient for 275 g / 12 oz / 3 cups of dried pasta).

Smoky Kale Crisps

Serves 2 as a snack

Tear the leaves from the ribs of 1 bunch washed and dried Tuscan kale into fairly large, chip-size pieces, then toss with about 2 tbsp olive oil, ½ tsp Spanish smoked paprika and about ½ tsp salt. Arrange the leaves in a single layer on a baking tray and bake in a 150°C (130°C fan) / 300F / gas 2 oven until dry and crisp.

Grilled Salmon with Spicy Melon Salsa

Serves: 4

Ingredients

90 g / 3 oz / ½ cup each honeydew, cantaloupe and watermelon, finely chopped

1 serrano chilli (chili), deseeded and minced

2 tbsp fresh coriander (cilantro), coarsely chopped

1 tbsp honey

2 tsp lime zest, grated

1 tsp fresh lime juice, or to taste

salt and freshly ground black pepper

750 g / 1 ½ lb wild salmon fillet, skin removed

1 tbsp canola oil, plus some for greasing

Method

1. In a bowl, stir together the melons, chilli, coriander, honey, lime zest and juice and a generous pinch each of salt and pepper. Mix well and let stand at room temperature for 15–30 minutes to allow the flavours to blend. Taste and adjust the seasoning with lime juice, salt and pepper. Set aside.

2. Prepare a grill for direct-heat cooking with a medium-high heat and lightly oil the grill rack. Alternatively, heat a griddle pan on the stove top and brush the pan with oil.

3. Sprinkle salt and pepper all over the salmon, then coat with 1 tbsp oil. Arrange the salmon on the grill and cook for 3–4 minutes, until nicely grill-marked on the first side. Turn and cook until browned on the second side and done to your liking.

4. Transfer the salmon to a platter and serve immediately with the melon salsa.

Halibut with Roasted Nectarine Chutney

Serves: 4

Ingredients

5 ripe yellow nectarines, halved, pitted and
coarsely chopped

1 tbsp olive oil, plus more for brushing

45 g / 1 ½ oz / ¼ cup golden raisins

2 tbsp red onion, minced

1 tsp fresh lemon juice

1 tsp light brown sugar

1 tsp fresh ginger, peeled and grated

4 halibut fillets

sea salt and freshly ground black pepper

fresh flat-leaf parsley, chopped, to garnish

Method

1. Preheat oven to 200°C (180°C fan) / 400F
/ gas 6.

2. In a baking dish, combine the nectarines,
1 tbsp olive oil, raisins, onion, lemon juice,
brown sugar and ginger. Stir to coat, then
spread evenly in the dish.

3. Brush the fillets with olive oil, then season
on both sides with salt and pepper. Place
the fillets on top of the nectarine mixture
and roast for 15–20 minutes, until the fish
is opaque throughout and flakes easily with
a fork and the fruit is tender.

4. To serve, place a fillet on each of four
warmed individual plates, top each with a
spoonful of the chutney and sprinkle with
parsley. Serve, placing the remaining
chutney on the table.

Prawn Tacos with Pineapple Salsa

Serves: 4

Ingredients

1 small pineapple, peeled, cored and diced

½ red onion, finely chopped

½ red bell pepper, deseeded and finely chopped

1 small cucumber, peeled, deseeded and diced

½ jalapeño chilli (chili), deseeded and finely chopped

20 g / ¾ oz / ½ cup fresh coriander (cilantro), chopped

2 tbsp fresh lime juice

2 tbsp extra-virgin olive oil

sea salt and freshly ground black pepper

2 tbsp grapeseed or canola oil, plus some for the grill

½ tsp chipotle chilli (chili) powder

1 small clove garlic, minced

500 g / 1 lb medium prawns (shrimp), peeled and deveined

8 small corn tortillas

Method

1. In a large bowl, combine the pineapple, onion, pepper, cucumber, jalapeño and coriander and toss together. Add the lime juice and olive oil. Season to taste, then stir. Cover and refrigerate until ready to serve.

2. Set the grill to a medium-high heat, then oil the grill. In a small bowl, mix together the grapeseed oil, chilli powder and garlic. Thread the prawns onto skewers and brush the prawns with some of the oil mixture.

3. Place the prawn skewers over the hottest part of the fire and grill for 2 minutes, until bright pink. Turn and cook for a further 2 minutes, until pink on the second side. The prawns should be firm to the touch at the thickest part. Transfer to a plate.

4. Lightly brush the tortillas with the remaining oil mixture and place over the hottest part of the grill. Grill for 1 minute on each side.

5. Place a tortilla on each of four individual plates, then arrange the prawns in the centre, dividing them evenly, and top each portion with the salsa. Serve immediately.

Turkey, Squash and Cranberry salad

Serves: 6

Ingredients

250 g / 8 oz / 1 ⅓ cups semi-pearled farro

1 ½ lb / 4 cups low-sodium chicken broth

sea salt and freshly ground black pepper

1 small butternut squash

8 tbsp extra-virgin olive oil

60 ml / 2 fl. oz / ¼ cup fresh lemon juice

1 tsp honey

1 tbsp fresh flat-leaf parsley, minced

185 g / 6 oz boneless smoked turkey, cut into 12 mm (½ in) cubes

90 g / 3 oz / ⅔ cup sweetened dried cranberries

3 green onions, white and tender green parts, thinly sliced

Method

1. Rinse the farro under cold water, then drain. In a saucepan, combine the farro, chicken broth and 1 tsp salt and bring to a boil over a high heat. Reduce the heat to medium-low and simmer, uncovered, for about 30 minutes, until all the liquid has absorbed. Transfer the farro to a large bowl.

2. Meanwhile, preheat the oven to 200°C (180°C fan) / 400F / gas 6. Remove the stem from the squash, then cut in half lengthwise. Scoop out the seeds and discard, then peel and cut the flesh into cubes. On a rimmed baking tray, toss the squash cubes with 2 tbsp of the oil, 1 tsp salt and ¼ tsp pepper. Roast for 12 minutes, until tender but still slightly firm. Allow to cool.

3. In a small bowl, whisk together the lemon juice, honey, parsley, ¼ tsp salt and some pepper. Slowly whisk in the remaining olive oil to make a dressing. Adjust the seasoning.

4. Add the dressing, squash, turkey, cranberries and green onions to the cooled farro and toss to mix well. Serve immediately.

Chicken with Balsamic Tomatoes

Serves: 4

Ingredients

4 chicken escalopes

sea salt and freshly ground black pepper

2 tbsp olive oil

1 or 2 large shallots, minced

1 clove garlic, minced

280 g / 9 oz / 1 ½ cups cherry and pear tomatoes, stemmed and halved

3 tbsp balsamic vinegar

15 g / ½ oz / ½ cup fresh basil leaves, torn

Method

1. Season the chicken escalopes generously on both sides with salt and pepper.

2. In a large frying pan, heat the olive oil over a medium-high heat. Add the chicken to the pan in batches and reduce the heat to medium. Cook for 4–5 minutes per side, turning once, until nicely browned and opaque throughout. Transfer each piece to a plate as it is finished and cover with kitchen foil to keep warm.

3. Add the shallots and garlic to the frying pan and cook for 3–4 minutes, stirring often, until softened. Add the tomatoes and vinegar. Cook for a further 4 minutes, still stirring often, until the tomatoes begin to soften and split. Stir in the basil and season with salt and pepper.

4. To serve, place a chicken breast on each of four plates and spoon the warm tomato salad on top. Serve immediately.

Spicy Ginger Beef and Pak Choi

Serves: 4

Ingredients

2 tbsp dry sherry

1 tbsp low-sodium soy sauce

½ tsp Asian red chilli (chili) paste, plus more
if desired

500 g / 1 lb baby pak choi (bok choy)

1 tbsp grapeseed or canola oil

2 cloves garlic, minced

1 tbsp fresh ginger, peeled and minced

500 g / 1 lb flank steak, thinly sliced across
the grain

Method

1. In a small bowl, stir together the sherry,
   soy sauce and chilli paste, then set aside.
   Trim the stem ends from the baby pak choi
   and separate into leaves.

2. In a wok or a large frying pan, heat ½ tbsp
   of the oil over a high heat until hot. Add the
   pak choi and cook for 2 minutes, stirring,
   just until tender-crisp. Transfer to a bowl.

3. Add the remaining oil to pan. When hot,
   add the garlic and ginger and cook for
   30 seconds, stirring often, until fragrant
   but not browned. Add the beef to the pan
   and cook for 2 minutes, tossing and stirring,
   until no longer pink.

4. Return the pak choi to the pan along with
   the sherry mixture and cook for 1 minute
   until heated through. If you like your food
   extra spicy, top with additional red chilli
   paste. Serve immediately.

Sides and Snacks

Enjoy flavourful, vibrant superfoods throughout the day and feel truly satisfied with every bite. These recipes are loaded with nutritious ingredients supplying you with essential minerals, vitamins and healthy fats.

Vegetables, herbs and spices are the main components in these wholesome recipes. The dishes can be served to accompany main meals or enjoyed as a snack anytime throughout the day.

Why not combine a few of the salads for a filling meal – ideal for lunchboxes, picnics and barbecues, too!

Braised Cabbage with Apples

Serves: 4–6

Ingredients

3 tbsp olive oil

1 yellow onion, thinly sliced

sea salt and freshly ground black pepper

1 tbsp honey

1 Granny Smith apple, halved, cored and thinly sliced

60 ml / 2 fl. oz / ¼ cup balsamic vinegar

250 ml / 8 fl. oz / 1 cup dry red wine

1 head red cabbage, cored and cut into thin shreds

1 orange, zest finely grated

Method

1. In a large frying pan, heat the olive oil over a medium heat. Add the onion and a pinch of salt and sauté for 5–7 minutes until the onion is soft and translucent. Add the honey and cook for a further minute. Add the apple slices and vinegar and raise the heat to medium-high. Bring the liquid to a boil, then add the wine and 250 ml / 8 fl. oz / 1 cup water. Season well and return to a boil. Reduce the heat to medium-low and simmer for about 10 minutes until the liquid begins to reduce.

2. Add the cabbage and toss to coat well with the liquid in the pan. Cover the pan and cook for 25–30 minutes, stirring occasionally, until the cabbage begins to wilt. Uncover and cook for a further 25–30 minutes until the cabbage is tender and most of the liquid has evaporated.

3. Season to taste. Remove the pan from the heat and stir in the orange zest, then transfer the cabbage to a bowl and serve.

Bacon Salad with Sprouts

Serves: 6

Ingredients

2 tbsp red wine vinegar

½ tsp grainy mustard

1 clove garlic, minced

60 ml / 2 fl. oz / ¼ cup extra-virgin olive oil

sea salt and freshly ground black pepper

750 g / 1 ½ lb Brussels sprouts

3 slices bacon, cooked until crisp and finely crumbled

Method

1. In a small bowl, whisk together the vinegar, mustard and garlic. Whisking constantly, pour in the olive oil in a slow, steady stream to make a vinaigrette. Season with salt and pepper and set aside.

2. Using a small, sharp knife, trim the bases of the Brussels sprouts. Remove and discard any blemished or discoloured leaves. Separate the leaves of the sprouts.

3. In a large saucepan over a medium heat, combine the Brussels sprout leaves and 125 ml / 4 fl. oz / ½ cup water. Cover and bring to a boil, then reduce the heat to medium-low and cook for about 7 minutes until the leaves are bright green and tender, adding more water if needed. Drain thoroughly and transfer to a serving bowl.

4. Drizzle the vinaigrette over the Brussels sprouts and toss to coat. Taste and adjust the seasoning. Sprinkle with the bacon and serve immediately.

Stir-fried Asparagus with Shiitakes

Serves: **4–6**

Ingredients

500 g / 1 lb asparagus, tough ends snapped off

3 tbsp canola or grapeseed oil

1 clove garlic, minced

1 tbsp fresh ginger, peeled and grated

185 g / 6 oz shiitake mushrooms, stems removed, caps brushed clean and thinly sliced

60 ml / 2 fl. oz / ¼ cup dry white wine or sake

60 ml / 2 fl. oz / ¼ cup low-sodium chicken broth

1 ½ tbsp low-sodium soy sauce

2 tsp sesame seeds

Method

1. Cut the asparagus on the diagonal into 5 cm (2 in) pieces.

2. In a large frying pan, heat the oil over a high heat. Add the garlic and ginger and cook for 30 seconds, stirring constantly until fragrant but not browned. Add the mushrooms and cook for 2 minutes, stirring often until they begin to brown, then add the asparagus and cook for 3 minutes, stirring constantly until bright green and tender.

3. Stir in the wine, broth and soy sauce and cook for 2–3 minutes, until the liquid is reduced to a sauce-like consistency and all the vegetables are tender. Stir in the sesame seeds, transfer to a dish and serve.

Cumin-roasted Sweet Potatoes

Serves: 4

Ingredients

2 orange-fleshed sweet potatoes, peeled

1 tbsp canola or grapeseed oil

1 tsp ground cumin

sea salt and freshly ground black pepper

2 tbsp fresh coriander (cilantro), finely chopped

Method

1. Preheat the oven to 200°C (180°C fan) / 400F / gas 6.

2. Cut the sweet potatoes crosswise into round discs. Rinse the discs under cold water and spread on a clean kitchen towel to dry.

3. Put the sweet potatoes in a bowl, then drizzle with the oil, sprinkle with the cumin and toss to coat evenly.

4. Preheat a baking tray in the oven for 5 minutes. Remove from the oven and carefully arrange the sweet potatoes in a single layer on the hot baking tray. Roast the sweet potatoes for 30–35 minutes, turning every 10 minutes, until evenly browned and tender when pierced with a knife.

5. Transfer the sweet potatoes to a warmed serving dish and sprinkle with ½ tsp salt, a grinding or two of pepper and the coriander. Toss gently to coat and serve immediately.

Sweet and Smoky Cauliflower

Serves: 4

Ingredients

2 tbsp unsalted butter

3 tbsp olive oil

1 large head cauliflower, cored and cut into 2.5 cm (1 in) florets

sea salt and freshly ground black pepper

1 shallot, minced

½ tsp smoked paprika

¼ tsp red pepper flakes

2 tbsp honey

½ lemon

Method

1. In a large frying pan over a medium heat, melt the butter with 2 tbsp of the olive oil. Add the cauliflower florets, sprinkle with a generous pinch of salt and coat the florets with the oil. Spread the florets in a single layer in the pan and cook for 3–4 minutes, without stirring, until lightly browned on the bottom. Turn each piece and continue cooking for 3–4 minutes, until browned on the second side. Repeat for 3–5 minutes until all sides are evenly browned.

2. Add the remaining olive oil, the shallot, paprika and red pepper flakes to the pan. Cook for 1–2 minutes, stirring occasionally, until the shallot is softened. Add the honey and 2 tbsp water and sauté for 2–3 minutes until the liquid reduces to a glaze. Squeeze the juice from the lemon half over the cauliflower, stir to combine, then cook for about 30 seconds. Remove from the heat. Season to taste.

3. Transfer the cauliflower to a warm bowl and serve immediately.

Roasted Ratatouille

Serves: 6–8

Ingredients

500 g / 1 lb plum tomatoes, halved lengthwise

4 large cloves garlic, sliced

1 large yellow onion, halved and cut crosswise into slices 6 mm (¼ in) thick

1 small aubergine (eggplant), trimmed and cut into 2.5 cm (1 in) chunks

1 small courgette (zucchini), trimmed and cut crosswise into 12 mm (½ in) slices

1 small yellow crookneck squash, trimmed and cut crosswise into 12 mm (½ in) slices

1 green bell pepper, deseeded and cut into 4 cm (1 ½ in) squares

5 tbsp olive oil

sea salt and freshly ground black pepper

10 g / ⅓ oz / ¼ cup fresh basil, finely shredded

2 tbsp fresh thyme, chopped

Method

1. Preheat the oven to 220°C (200°C fan) / 425F / gas 7.

2. Combine the tomatoes, garlic, onion, aubergine, courgette, yellow squash and pepper in a large bowl. Drizzle in the olive oil, sprinkle generously with salt and toss to coat. Transfer the vegetables to a large baking tray and spread in an even layer.

3. Roast the vegetables, stirring once or twice, for 20 minutes. Remove from the oven and sprinkle with the basil and thyme. Continue to roast for 5–10 minutes, again stirring once or twice, until the biggest pieces are tender when pierced with a fork. Remove the vegetables from the oven and season with salt and pepper.

4. Transfer the ratatouille to a bowl. Serve hot, warm, or at room temperature.

Four Ways to Use Tomatoes

Tomatoes are abundant at the market during summer and early autumn. Since they are such nutritional powerhouses, use them often. Cooking tomatoes makes lycopene, a powerful antioxidant, easier for the body to use.

Roasted Tomatoes

Makes about 500 g / 16 oz / 2 cups

Cut 1.5 kg / 3 lb heirloom tomatoes in half and place cut-side up on a baking tray. In a small bowl, mix together 1 tbsp olive oil, 2 tbsp balsamic vinegar, 1 minced garlic clove, ¼ tsp each salt and freshly ground black pepper and the leaves from 1 sprig fresh thyme. Spoon the mixture evenly over the tomatoes and bake in a 160°C (140°C fan) / 325F / gas 3 oven for 1 hour, until the tomatoes are soft and wrinkled. Add to pastas, vegetable dishes, sandwiches and pizzas.

Tomato Pesto

Makes about 250 g / 8 oz / 1 cup

Place 45 g / 1 ½ oz / ½ cup sun-dried tomatoes in a heatproof bowl, add boiling water to cover and stand for 15 minutes to re-hydrate. Drain, then add to a food processor along with 2 diced plum tomatoes, 20 g / ¾ oz / ½ cup fresh basil leaves, 1 chopped garlic clove and ½ tsp salt, then pulse until puréed. With the motor running, slowly drizzle in 2 tbsp extra-virgin olive oil until blended. Use on pizzas, or with pastas or vegetables.

Cannellini Beans with Tomatoes and Basil

Serves 4

In a bowl, mix together 470 g / 15 oz / 2 cans cannellini beans, rinsed and drained, 2 deseeded and chopped tomatoes, ¼ cup finely chopped red onion, 2 tbsp balsamic vinegar, 1 tbsp extra-virgin olive oil, 3 tbsp torn fresh basil leaves and salt and pepper to taste. Allow to stand for 30 minutes or refrigerate for up to 4 hours before serving.

Heirloom Tomatoes with Sherry Vinaigrette

Serves 4

In a small bowl, whisk together 3 tbsp extra-virgin olive oil, 1 tbsp sherry vinegar, 1 minced large shallot and salt and pepper to taste. Core 500 g / 1 lb heirloom tomatoes and cut into thin wedges. Arrange on a platter, drizzle with the vinaigrette and serve sprinkled with chopped fresh herbs.

Sautéed Peas with Basil and Pecorino

Serves: 4

Ingredients

1 tbsp unsalted butter

1 tbsp olive oil

250 g / ½ lb sugar snap peas, strings removed

500 g / 1 lb garden peas, shelled

sea salt and freshly ground black pepper

1 lemon

leaves from 4 fresh basil sprigs, torn

30 g / 1 oz chunk pecorino Romano cheese

Method

1. In a large frying pan over a medium heat, melt the butter with the olive oil. Add the sugar snap and garden peas. Pour in 60 ml / 2 fl. oz / ¼ cup water and add a pinch of salt. Cover and cook for 2 minutes. Uncover and cook for another 2 minutes, stirring occasionally, until the water has evaporated. The peas should be tender-crisp and still bright green.

2. Finely grate 2 tsp zest from the lemon, then halve the lemon. Remove the pan from the heat and squeeze the juice from 1 lemon half over the peas (reserve the remaining half for another use). Add the lemon zest, basil and a pinch each of salt and pepper to the pan. Grate cheese over the top to taste and stir to mix well. Transfer the peas to a warm serving dish and serve immediately.

Squash and Pears with Rosemary

Serves: 4

Ingredients

1 Bosc pear

1 tbsp grapeseed or canola oil

½ small butternut squash, peeled, deseeded
   and thinly sliced

sea salt

1 tbsp fresh rosemary, finely chopped

a pinch of cayenne pepper

125 ml / 4 fl. oz / ½ cup apple juice

Method

1. Halve and core the pear and cut it lengthwise
   into thin slices.

2. In a frying pan, heat the oil over a medium-
   high heat. Add the squash and sprinkle with
   1 tsp salt. Cook for about 5 minutes, stirring
   often, until the squash is browned on the
   edges and begins to soften.

3. Add the pear, rosemary, cayenne and apple
   juice and cook for 6–8 minutes until the liquid
   evaporates and the squash is tender. Transfer
   to a serving bowl. Serve hot, warm or at
   room temperature.

Moroccan Carrot and Parsnip Salad

Serves: 6

Ingredients

¼ tsp ground cinnamon

¼ tsp ground cumin

¼ tsp ground coriander

⅛ tsp ground ginger

3 large carrots

3 large parsnips

60 ml / 2 fl. oz / ¼ cup fresh lemon juice

1 tbsp honey

¾ tsp prepared harissa

sea salt and freshly ground black pepper

6 tbsp extra-virgin olive oil

60 g / 2 oz / ½ cup roasted shelled pistachio nuts, coarsely chopped

125 g / 4 oz / ⅔ cup raisins

10 g / ⅓ oz / ¼ cup fresh coriander (cilantro) or mint, coarsely chopped

Method

1. In a frying pan over a medium-low heat, combine the cinnamon, cumin, coriander and ginger and toast for 2 minutes, stirring constantly, until fragrant. Remove from the heat and let cool to room temperature.

2. Peel and grate the carrots and parsnips. Set aside.

3. In a small bowl, whisk together the toasted spices, lemon juice, honey, harissa and a scant ½ tsp salt. Slowly whisk in the olive oil to make a dressing. Adjust the seasoning.

4. In a bowl, stir together the pistachios and a pinch of salt. Add the carrots and parsnips, raisins, ½ tsp salt, several grindings of pepper and the dressing, then toss well. Taste and adjust the seasoning.

5. Transfer to a platter or serving bowl, sprinkle with the coriander and serve.

Desserts

It's always tempting to finish a meal with a sweet treat, but all too often desserts are laden with refined sugars, nasty preservatives and dairy products. This can be avoided with fresh ingredients, seasonal fruits and natural sugars. There are a number of healthy, guilt-free dessert options, you just have to think outside the box.

This chapter includes a variety of fresh, vibrant and decadent treats to finish off a super-healthy feast. Impress guests with the hearty winter cobbler, deliciously dark chocolate mousse or cooling granita – perfect for a summer's evening.

You'll be surprised at how many naughty desserts can be made healthier by replacing a few ingredients and cooking from scratch. Plan ahead for easy, stress-free baking – careful prepping really does make a difference!

Three-berry Cobbler

Serves: 6

Ingredients

canola oil spray

250 g / 8 oz / 2 cups blueberries

500 g / 1 lb / 4 cups raspberries

500 g / 1 lb / 4 cups strawberries, hulled and
halved lengthwise

75 g / 2 ½ oz / ¼ cup raspberry jam (jelly)

1 tbsp instant tapioca

75 g / 2 ½ oz / ½ cup wholewheat flour

75 g / 2 ½ oz / ½ cup plain (all-purpose) flour

2 tsp baking powder

¼ tsp bicarbonate of (baking) soda

½ tsp sea salt

3 tbsp unsalted butter, at room temperature

90 g / 3 oz / ⅓ cup sugar

80 ml / 3 fl. oz / ⅓ cup fat-free buttermilk

Method

1. Preheat the oven to 180°C (160°C fan) /
   350F / gas 4. Coat a medium square baking
   dish lightly with the canola oil spray.

2. For the filling, combine the blueberries,
   raspberries, strawberries, jam and tapioca
   in a bowl. Stir gently to coat the berries with
   the jam. Spread the fruit in an even layer in
   the prepared pan.

3. To make the topping, whisk together the
   flours, baking powder, bicarbonate of soda
   and salt in a bowl. In a separate bowl, beat
   together the butter and sugar for 3 minutes
   until fluffy. Beat in half of the buttermilk, then
   add half of the dry ingredients and combine.
   Add the remaining buttermilk. Add the
   remaining dry ingredients and beat until
   a thick batter forms. Do not overmix.

4. Drop the batter by heaping spoonfuls over
   the fruit. Spread it as evenly as possible,
   using the back of the spoon.

5. Bake the cobbler for 40 minutes until the
   crust is deep golden brown. Allow to cool
   slightly before serving.

Cantaloupe-basil Granita

Serves: 8

Ingredients

30 fresh basil leaves
60 ml / 2 fl. oz / ¼ cup fresh lime juice
155 g / 5 oz / ⅓ cup sugar
1 ripe cantaloupe

Method

1. Coarsely chop 20 basil leaves and set the remaining leaves aside. In a saucepan over a medium-high heat, combine the lime juice, sugar and 2 tbsp water. Simmer for 2 minutes, swirling occasionally, until the sugar is dissolved. Remove from the heat, then stir in the chopped basil, cover, and allow steep for 15 minutes.

2. Meanwhile, halve the cantaloupe and scoop out and discard the seeds. Cut off the rind, and cut the flesh into cubes.

3. Strain the basil mixture through a fine-mesh sieve into a blender. Add half of the melon cubes and pulse, then purée until smooth. Add the remaining melon cubes and pulse, then add the reserved whole basil leaves and purée until the mixture is smooth. Pour the mixture into a rectangular baking dish. Cover with cling film, place on a baking sheet and place in the freezer.

4. Leave overnight. The mixture should be completely frozen with a fluffy texture. Spoon the granita into bowls and serve.

Olive Oil Chocolate Mousse

Serves: 4

Ingredients

185 g / 6 oz dark chocolate,
  finely chopped

3 large egg yolks

60 ml / 2 fl. oz / ¼ cup extra-virgin olive oil

3 tbsp warm water

¼ tsp sea salt

2 large egg whites

⅛ tsp cream of tartar

60 g / 2 oz / ¼ cup sugar

chocolate shavings to serve (optional)

Method

1. In a heatproof bowl set over a pan of barely simmering water, stir the chocolate until melted and smooth. Remove from the heat and whisk in the egg yolks, olive oil, warm water and salt until well blended.

2. In a clean bowl, beat the egg whites with the cream of tartar until frothy. Add the sugar and continue beating until the mixture forms soft peaks. Fold one-third into the chocolate mixture combined, then gently fold in the remaining egg-white mixture until well incorporated.

3. Spoon the mousse evenly into four custard cups and refrigerate until well chilled, at least 4 hours or overnight. Sprinkle with the chocolate shavings and serve immediately.

Note: This recipe contains raw eggs. If you have health and safety concerns, you may wish to avoid foods made with raw eggs.

Roasted Spiced Black Plums

Serves: 4–6

Ingredients

canola oil spray

8 ripe black plums, halved and pitted

1 tbsp brown sugar

8 star anise pods

fat-free or low-fat vanilla frozen yogurt for serving

Method

1. Preheat the oven to 200°C (180°C fan) / 400F / gas 6. Coat a large baking dish with the canola oil spray.

2. Arrange the plums, cut side up, in the prepared dish. Cut a thin slice off the round side of each half to help them sit flat. Sprinkle brown sugar over each plum half, dividing evenly, then sprinkle the star anise pods evenly over the top.

3. Roast for 15 minutes until the sugar has melted, the plums are warmed through and the skins are just beginning to wrinkle a bit on the edges. Serve once cooled or eat warm.

4. To serve, put scoops of frozen yogurt in four dessert bowls, arrange 2 plum halves on top of each (discard the star anise), and serve immediately.

Nectarines with Cinnamon Streusel

Serves: 4

Ingredients

canola oil spray

4 ripe but firm nectarines, halved and pitted

6 tbsp wholewheat flour

6 tbsp brown sugar

½ tsp ground cinnamon

⅛ tsp sea salt

2 tbsp unsalted butter, cut into pieces

60 g / 2 oz / ⅓ cup roasted almonds, chopped

Method

1. Preheat the oven to 200°C (180°C fan) / 400F / gas 6. Coat a medium-sized rectangular baking dish lightly with the canola oil spray.

2. Arrange the nectarines, cut side up, in the prepared dish. Cut a thin slice off the round side to help them sit flat. Set aside.

3. In a food processor, combine the flour, brown sugar, cinnamon and salt and pulse a few times to mix. Add the butter pieces and pulse until the mixture resembles coarse crumbs. Do not overmix. Stir in the almonds, then squeeze the mixture into small handfuls and distribute it evenly over the nectarine halves, pressing it lightly to adhere.

4. Bake for 20 minutes, until the nectarines are tender when pierced with a small knife and the topping has browned, then arrange 2 nectarine halves on each of four dessert plates and serve warm.

Roasted Pears with Honey

Serves: 6

Ingredients

45 g / ½ oz / ⅓ cup flaked (slivered)
  almonds
3 ripe but firm Bosc pears
140 ml / 4 ½ fl. oz / ⅓ cup honey
4 bay leaves
3 tbsp unsalted butter, cut into 6 pieces
2 tbsp amaretto liqueur
375 g / 12 oz / 1 ½ cups fat-free or low-fat
  plain Greek-style yogurt

Method

1. Preheat the oven to 190°C (170°C fan) /
   375F / gas 5. Lightly toast the almonds in
   a saucepan for a few minutes. Pour onto
   a plate to cool, leaving the oven on.

2. Halve the pears lengthways. Using a melon
   baller, scoop out the cores. In a heavy
   ovenproof saucepan, combine the honey
   and bay leaves. Bring to a simmer over a
   medium-high heat. Reduce the heat, stirring
   occasionally until the honey changes colour.
   Remove from the heat.

3. Place the butter pieces in the pot with the
   honey, spacing them evenly. Place a pear
   half, cut side down, on top of each piece of
   butter. Cover the pot and roast the pears in
   the oven for 10 minutes, then turn over. Baste
   the pears with the honey mixture. Drizzle the
   pears with the amaretto and continue to roast
   for 6–8 minutes until golden brown. Remove
   from the oven and let the pears cool slightly.

4. Whisk the yogurt in a bowl until smooth.
   Arrange the pear halves on a platter, drizzle
   the honey mixture from the pot over the top
   and sprinkle with the toasted almonds.

Four Ways to Use Pears

Adaptable pears go well with a range of different ingredients. Try them raw as a sweet contrast to tart cranberries in a fresh relish, or sliced as part of a salad. Roasted, pears complement sweet vegetables and help offset savoury meats and poultry with their bright flavour.

Pear, Orange and Cranberry Relish

Makes about 1 l / 32 fl. oz / 4 cups

In a food processor, process 1 navel orange, halved and cut into thin wedges (including peel), 3 cups cranberries and 2–3 tbsp sugar, until finely chopped. Transfer to a bowl and stir in 2 firm but ripe pears, peeled, cored and finely chopped, and ½ tsp ground cardamom. Mix well and refrigerate for about 1 hour before serving. Serve with roasted poultry or meat.

Pear and Fennel Salad

Serves 4

In a large bowl, whisk together 1 tbsp sherry vinegar, 2 tbsp extra-virgin olive oil, 1 tbsp coarsely grated pecorino Romano cheese and salt and pepper to taste. Add 1 bulb fennel, shaved, and toss to coat. Arrange 45 g / 1 ½ oz / 1 ½ cups rocket (arugula) leaves on each plate and top with some fennel mixture. Top each salad with ½ pear, halved, cored and thinly sliced. Sprinkle each with 1 tbsp dried currants.

Pears and Parsnips with Almonds

Serves 6

On a rimmed baking tray, arrange 500 g / 1 lb parsnips, peeled and quartered, and 3 Bosc or Anjou pears, quartered lengthwise and cored. Sprinkle with 3 tbsp olive oil and salt to taste, then toss to coat evenly. Spread out in an even layer and roast in a 200°C (180°C fan) / 400F / gas 6 oven for 30–40 minutes until tender and browned. Top with 3 tbsp toasted almonds and serve.

Savoury Roasted Pears

Serves 4 as a side dish

Oil a shallow baking dish and drizzle 1 tbsp maple syrup into the dish. Arrange 4 firm but ripe Bosc, Bartlett or Anjou pears, halved lengthways and cored in the dish, cut-side up. Brush the cut sides with fresh lemon juice and sprinkle with 1 tbsp chopped fresh sage. Drizzle the pears with 2 tbsp dry white wine. Roast in a 220°C (200°C fan) / 425F / gas 7 oven for 22–25 minutes until tender. Serve warm or at room temperature drizzled with the pan juices.

Spiced Mango Pavlovas

Serves: 6

Ingredients

5 whole green cardamom pods

125 g / 4 oz / ½ cups sugar

3 ripe mangoes, peeled and cut into 12 mm (½ in) cubes

1 lime, juiced and zest finely grated

6 ready-made meringues

whipped cream, to serve

Method

1. Crack open the cardamom pods. Add the pods to a saucepan along with the sugar and 2 tbsp water and simmer for 2 minutes. Allow to cool.

2. Place the mangoes in a bowl. Squeeze the lime juice over the mangoes, pour the cardamom syrup through a fine-mesh sieve into the bowl and stir to mix well.

3. Place each of the meringues on a dessert plate. Spoon a small amount of whipped cream on top of each meringue. Using a slotted spoon, top the whipped cream with some of the mango cubes. Drizzle a little cardamom syrup over the top, sprinkle with lime zest and serve immediately.

Basics

These staple recipes include flavourful dressings, sauces, condiments and seasonings that will enhance a variety of dishes. Use them as part of any healthy meal.

Pico de Gallo

3 tomatoes

½ red onion

2–4 serrano chillies (chilies)

1 tbsp finely chopped fresh coriander (cilantro)

2 tsp fresh lime juice

sea salt

1. Finely chop the tomatoes and onion into equal-size pieces. Seed and mince the chillies.

2. In a large bowl, stir together the tomatoes, onion, chillies, coriander, lime juice and 2 tsp salt. Allow the salsa stand for 1 hour.

3. Serve right away, or cover and store in the refrigerator for up to 3 days.

4. Makes about 375 ml / 12 fl. oz / 1 ½ cups.

Gremolata

30 g / 1 oz / ⅔ cup flat-leaf parsley, chopped

finely grated zest of 1 lemon

2 cloves garlic, minced

1. In a small bowl, stir together the parsley, lemon zest and garlic. Serve over cooked fish, chicken, meat or steamed vegetables.

2. Makes about ¾ cup (1½ oz / 45 g).

Romesco Dressing

2 tbsp extra-virgin olive oil

1 tbsp fresh orange juice

2 tbsp sherry vinegar

¼ tsp Spanish sweet smoked paprika

2 cloves garlic, minced

3 jarred piquillo peppers, drained

1 ½ tbsp chopped blanched almonds

sea salt and freshly ground black pepper

1. In a food processor, combine the olive oil, orange juice, vinegar, paprika, garlic, piquillo peppers, almonds, a scant ½ tsp salt and a few grindings of pepper. Process until a relatively smooth dressing forms, about 15 seconds. Taste and adjust the seasoning.

2. Makes about 180 ml / 6 fl. oz / ¾ cup.

Sun-dried Tomato Vinaigrette

4 sun-dried tomato halves

boiling water as needed

60 ml / 2 fl. oz / ¼ cup extra-virgin olive oil

3 tbsp fresh lemon juice

1 tbsp flat-leaf parsley, finely chopped

1 tbsp fresh dill, finely chopped

1 tsp grated orange zest

1 small clove garlic, minced

sea salt and freshly ground black pepper

1. Place the sun-dried tomatoes in a heatproof bowl, pour over boiling water to cover, and let stand for 5 minutes. Drain the tomatoes and finely dice. In a small bowl, whisk together the olive oil, lemon juice, sun-dried tomatoes, parsley, dill, orange zest, garlic, 2 tbsp water, ½ tsp salt and a generous grinding of pepper until blended.

2. Makes about 180 ml / 6 fl. oz / ¾ cup.

Pesto

1 tbsp pine nuts

125 ml / 4 fl. oz / ½ cup extra-virgin olive oil

2 large cloves garlic

sea salt and freshly ground black pepper

45 g / 1 ½ oz / 1 ½ cups fresh basil leaves

15 g / ½ oz / ¼ cup spinach leaves, coarsely chopped

2 tbsp freshly grated Parmesan cheese

1. In a dry frying pan, toast the nuts until lightly browned and fragrant, about 3 minutes; watch carefully, as they burn easily. Immediately pour onto a plate to stop the cooking and let cool.

2. In a food processor, combine the olive oil, pine nuts, garlic and ½ tsp salt. Pulse, scraping down the sides as needed, until fairly smooth. Add the basil, spinach and ¼ tsp pepper and process until blended, but with some texture. Transfer to a glass or ceramic bowl and stir in the cheese.

3. Makes about 250 ml / 8 fl. oz / 1 cup.

Glossary

Antibacterial: Helping to destroy or inhibit the growth of bacteria. Ingredients with antibacterial properties include garlic and some fresh herbs, such as peppermint.

Anti-inflammatory: Helping to reduce or prevent inflammation in the body tissues. Anti-inflammatory ingredients include deeply pigmented fruits and vegetables, spices such as turmeric, and fresh herbs.

Antimicrobial: Helping to destroy or inhibit the growth of microbes, such as salmonella. Ingredients with antimicrobial properties include some alliums and fresh herbs like basil and coriander.

Antioxidants: Antioxidants protect against and repair daily damage to our cells and tissues. They have also been linked to heart health and cancer prevention. The best sources of antioxidants are colourful fruits, vegetables, nuts and wholegrains.

Carbohydrates: There are three main kinds of carbohydrates: starch, sugar and fibre. Starch and sugar provide our bodies and brains with energy. Although our bodies can't digest fibre, it provides a number of significant benefits. The healthiest sources of carbohydrates are fruits, vegetables, beans and wholegrains.

Carotenoids: Carotenoids are coloured pigments in plants that provide multiple health benefits such as improved vision and enhanced immunity.

Cholesterol: Foods from animal sources such as eggs, milk, cheese and meat contain cholesterol, but the human body makes its own supply as well. Foods rich in saturated fat raise unhealthy LDL cholesterol in our blood streams more substantially than cholesterol from other food. Plant compounds like phytosterols in wheat germ, peanuts and almonds and beta-glucan from oats have been shown to lower cholesterol.

Fats: Our bodies need fat to absorb certain vitamins, build the membranes that line our cells, and cushion our joints and organs. Saturated and hydrogenated fats are linked to chronic ailments such as heart disease, while unsaturated fats can be more healthy.

Monounsaturated fats: Found in nuts, avocados, olive oil and canola oil, these fats are less likely to raise levels of unhealthy LDL cholesterol, linked to heart attack and stroke. They also help keep arteries clear by maintaining healthy HDL cholesterol.

Polyunsaturated fats: These fats play an important role in helping control cholesterol. While most of us get plenty of the polyunsaturated fat linolenic acid from vegetable, corn, and soybean oil, our diets don't usually contain enough of heart-healthy omega-3 fats. These are found as EPA and DHA in fish or in the form of alpha linolenic acid in flaxseed, canola oil and walnuts.

Saturated fats: Found in meats, dairy products and tropical oils such as coconut oil and palm oil, these fats can raise blood levels of unhealthy LDL cholesterol.

Trans fats: Present in hydrogenated vegetable oils in many processed and fried foods, trans fats may be even more harmful than saturated fats.

Fibre: Fibre is the component of plant foods that our bodies can't digest. Insoluble fibre does not dissolve in water and is known for preventing constipation. Soluble fibre softens in water and helps lower blood cholesterol levels.

Flavonoids: These plant compounds help prevent heart disease. They include quercetin from onions and apples, anthocyanidins from berries and isoflavones from soy.

Free radicals: These unstable molecules act to damage healthy cells and to cause inflammation in body tissues. Eating antioxidants can help counteract their damage.

Glycaemic index: A method of measuring the effects of various foods on blood sugar. Foods that quickly raise blood sugar levels rate high on the index, while foods that slowly act on blood sugar rate near the bottom. Foods that produce a slow but sustained release of sugar in the bloodstream are considered best for optimum health.

Lycopene: A carotenoid believed to protect against heart disease and some types of cancer. It is found in tomatoes and other red fruits and vegetables.

Minerals: Minerals are elements that our bodies need in varying quantities for survival. Major minerals, such as calcium, are required in larger amounts, while trace minerals like iron and zinc are required in smaller amounts.

> *Calcium:* Vital for bone health, calcium is also important for muscle contraction and blood pressure regulation. Calcium-rich foods include low-fat milk, fish and vegetables such as broccoli and spinach.

> *Chromium:* A trace element that is important for metabolism and insulin function in the body.

> *Copper:* This trace mineral is essential for proper iron processing. It is also involved in healing and metabolism.

> *Folate:* Folate helps produce and maintain new cell growth.

> *Iron:* This mineral helps the body transport and use oxygen, and also plays a role in immune function, temperature regulation, cognitive development and energy metabolism.

> *Manganese:* This trace mineral is needed for proper metabolism of carbohydrates, fats and proteins. It also keeps bones and teeth healthy.

> *Phosphorus:* Phosphorus helps build strong bones and teeth, and helps the body get energy from food.

> *Potassium:* Potassium helps the body maintain water and mineral balance, and regulates heartbeat and blood pressure.

> *Zinc:* Zinc promotes a healthy immune system and supports optimal growth and reproduction.

Phytochemicals: These plant-based compounds have a positive effect on the body. Deeply pigmented fruits and vegetables tend to be highest in phytochemicals, but they are also found in tea, chocolate and nuts. Familiar phytonutrient groups include carotenoids and polyphenols.

Polyphenols: A class of antioxidant chemicals present in deeply pigmented fruits and vegetables as well as tea, which may help protect the heart.

Protein: Made of amino acids, protein provides the building blocks our bodies need to synthesize cells, tissues, hormones and antibodies. It is found in foods of animal and vegetable origin, although animal proteins contain more of the amino acids our bodies need to synthesize protein.

Vitamins: Our bodies require vitamins in order to function properly. They fall into two categories: fat-soluble vitamins, which require fat for absorption and are stored in our body's fat tissue, and water-soluble vitamins, which cannot be stored and must be replenished often.

Vitamin A: Found in dairy products, yellow-orange fruits and vegetables, and dark green leafy vegetables, vitamin A promotes healthy skin, hair, bones and vision. It also works as an antioxidant.

B vitamins: This group of water-soluble vitamins can be found in a range of fruits and vegetables, wholegrains, and dairy and meat products and includes vitamins B6 and B12, biotin, niacin, pantothenic acid, thiamin, folate and riboflavin. Each one plays a vital role in bodily functions.

Vitamin C: This water-soluble vitamin helps build body tissues, fights infection, helps keep gums healthy, and helps the body absorb iron. It also works as an antioxidant. It can be found in many fruits and vegetables, especially citrus.

Vitamin D: Instrumental in building and maintaining healthy bones and teeth, vitamin D can be found in fish such as salmon and sardines, as well as in fortified milk and cereal.

Vitamin E: Found in nuts and seeds, wholegrains, dark green vegetables and beans, vitamin E helps form red blood cells, prevents oxidation of LDL cholesterol, and improves immunity.

Vitamin K: Necessary for protein synthesis as well as blood clotting, vitamin K can be found in dark green vegetables, asparagus and cabbage.

Individual ingredient images, pages 32–121

© iStock / Getty

All other images © Weldon Owen